MINIBEASTS UP CLOSE

Grasshoppers Up Close

Greg Pyers

Raintree

First published 2005 by Heinemann Library
a division of Harcourt Education Australia,
18–22 Salmon Street, Port Melbourne Victoria 3207 Australia
(a division of Reed International Books Australia Pty Ltd,
ABN 70 001 002 357).
Visit the Heinemann Library website at
www.heinemannlibrary.com.au

Published in Great Britain by Raintree,
Halley Court, Jordan Hill, Oxford OX2 8EJ,
part of Harcourt Education
Raintree is a registered trademark of Harcourt Education Ltd.

ℝ A Reed Elsevier company

© Reed International Books Australia Pty Ltd 2005

09 08 07 06 05
10 9 8 7 6 5 4 3 2 1

Editorial: Anne McKenna, Carmel Heron
Design: Kerri Wilson, Stella Vassiliou
Photo research: Legend Images, Wendy Duncan
Production: Tracey Jarrett
Illustration: Rob Mancini

Typeset in Officina Sans 19/23 pt
Film separations by Digital Imaging Group (DIG), Melbourne
Printed and bound in Hong Kong and China by South China
Printing Company Ltd.

The paper used to print this book comes from sustainable
resources.

National Library of Australia Cataloguing-in-Publication data:

Pyers, Greg.
    Grasshoppers up close.

    Includes index.
    For primary school students.
    ISBN 1 74070 230 1.

    1. Grasshoppers – Juvenile literature. I. Title.
    (Series: Minibeasts up close).

595.726

Acknowledgements
The publisher would like to thank the following for permission
to reproduce photographs: Auscape/John Cancalosi: p. **21**,
/Mike Gillam: p. **5**, /Pascal Goetgheluck: p. **6**, /C. Andrew
Henley: p. **28**, /Wayne Lawler: p. **4**; Australian Picture
Library/Corbis: pp. **22, 24**; © Bill Beatty: p. **25**; © Bradley
Ireland Productions: p. **20**; Denis Crawford – Graphic Science:
p. **23**; © Dwight Kuhn: pp. **28–29**; Copyright Dennis Kunkel
Microscopy, Inc.: p. **12**; Lochman Transparencies/Jiri Lochman:
p. **10**; photolibrary.com: pp. **8, 14, 15, 16, 17**, /IndexStock:
p. **7**, /Gianni Tortoli: p. **26**; © Paul Zborowski: pp. **11, 13**.

Cover photograph of a south-eastern lubber grasshopper
reproduced with the permission of photolibrary.com/Animals
Animals/Patti Murray.

Every attempt has been made to trace and acknowledge
copyright. Where an attempt has been unsuccessful, the
publisher would be pleased to hear from the copyright
owner so any omission or error can be rectified.

Contents

Words that are printed in bold, **like this**, are explained in the glossary on page 31.

Amazing grasshoppers!

Have you ever seen a grasshopper? Perhaps you have noticed a grasshopper's long jumping legs, bent up over its back. With a sudden push, these legs shoot the grasshopper into the air. When you look at them up close, grasshoppers really are amazing animals.

If you look closely, you may see a grasshopper climbing a plant.

What are grasshoppers?

Grasshoppers are insects. Insects have six legs and no bones inside their bodies. Instead, their bodies have a hard, waterproof skin. This skin is called an **exoskeleton**.

Long-horned grasshoppers have very long feelers called **antennae** (an-<u>ten</u>-ay). Short-horned grasshoppers have short antennae.

The long-horned grasshopper is one of more than 9000 kinds, or **species**, of grasshoppers.

Protection from predators

When a grasshopper is picked up, it may dribble a dark green **liquid** from its mouth. **Predators**, such as birds, find the smell and taste of this liquid unpleasant and leave the grasshopper alone.

5

Where do grasshoppers live?

Any warm place with leafy plants and shelter may have grasshoppers living there.

Habitat

A **habitat** is a place where an animal lives. Grassy fields, wheat crops and bushes are good habitats for grasshoppers. Short-horned grasshoppers usually live close to the ground. Long-horned grasshoppers are most likely to be found climbing among bushes.

Short-horned grasshoppers climb along grass stems to feed.

When basking, grasshoppers choose a place sheltered from the wind and they sit still.

Getting warm

Grasshoppers cannot be active unless their bodies are warm. So, in the morning, grasshoppers **bask** in the sun. When its body is warm enough, a grasshopper can move around and feed.

In the middle of the day, when it is hot, grasshoppers may find shade. In warm climates, grasshoppers can be active all year. In places that have cold winters, grasshoppers are active only during the warm months.

Grasshopper body parts

A grasshopper's body has three main parts. These are the head, the **thorax** and the **abdomen** (<u>ab</u>-da-men).

The head

The head has mouthparts, two feelers called **antennae** and two eyes.

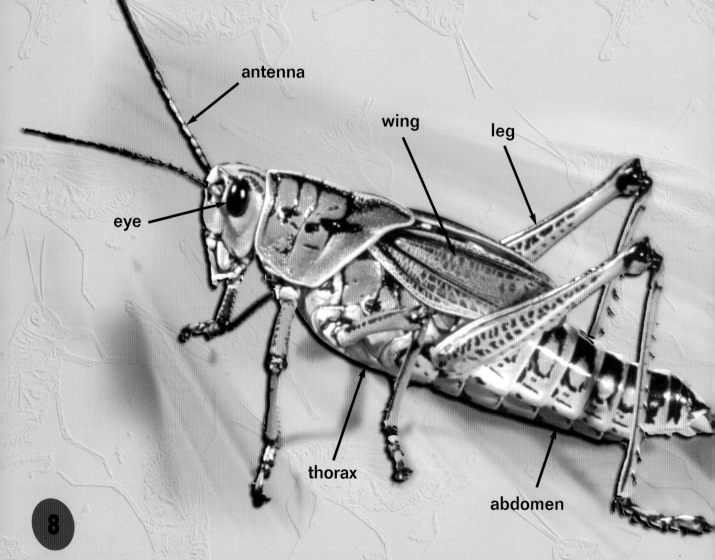

antenna

wing

leg

eye

thorax

abdomen

The thorax

A grasshopper's legs are attached to the thorax. Most grasshoppers have two or four wings also attached to the thorax. The thorax has strong muscles inside it to work the legs and wings.

The abdomen

A grasshopper's abdomen has eleven segments, or parts, that fit together loosely. This lets the abdomen bend. A female grasshopper produces eggs in her abdomen.

Colour and shape

Most grasshoppers have body colours and patterns that blend with their surroundings. Grasshoppers that live in grass are often green and brown. They may also have pointed heads and long bodies. This makes it difficult for **predators** to see them.

Mouthparts and eating

Tender, juicy shoots and young leaves make up most of a grasshopper's diet.

Grasshopper food

Some grasshopper **species** eat mainly flowers. Flowers are very easy to chew. They also have **pollen** and **nectar**, which provide a lot of energy.

Some long-horned grasshoppers also eat animals, such as aphids, worms, snails and even young grasshoppers.

This grasshopper, a spur-throated locust, is eating a prickly plant.

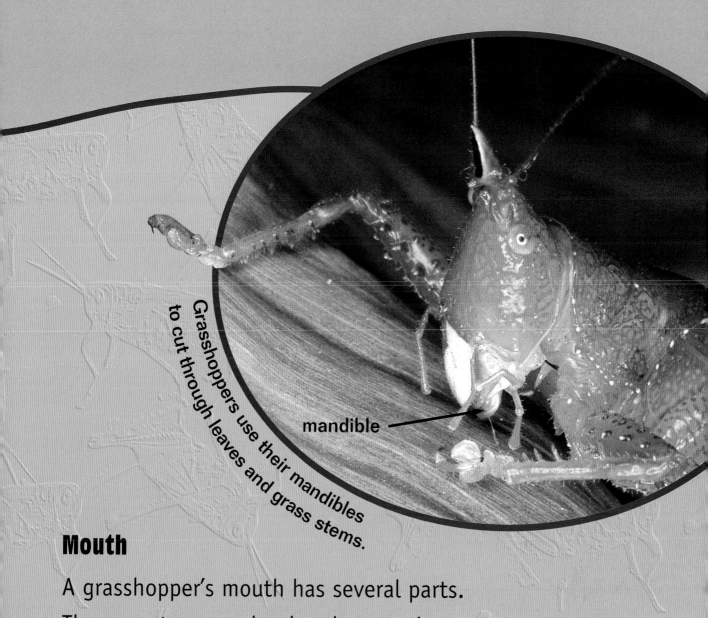

Grasshoppers use their mandibles to cut through leaves and grass stems.

mandible

Mouth

A grasshopper's mouth has several parts. There are two very hard and strong jaws, called **mandibles**. Strong muscles make the mandibles open and close from side to side.

On each side of a grasshopper's mouth are two **palps**. The palps look and work like fingers, moving food to the mandibles. A grasshopper uses its front feet to hold food.

Eyes and ears

Grasshoppers can see and hear. But not in the same way we do.

Eyes

A grasshopper has two large **compound eyes**. Each compound eye is made up of thousands of very small eyes. Each small eye faces in a slightly different direction. Together, the small eyes give a grasshopper an excellent view to the front, side and back.

A grasshopper also has three small eyes called **ocelli** (oh-s<u>ell</u>y) on the top of its head. These see only light and dark.

This close-up photo shows how the small eyes of a grasshopper's compound eye fit tightly together.

Ears

The ears of a long-horned grasshopper are in the front legs, just below the knees. Sound passes through a slit in each leg and enters the ear.

The ears of a short-horned grasshopper are in the first part, or segment, of the grasshopper's **abdomen**. There is one ear on each side. Each ear is covered by a thin skin.

Grasshopper hearing

Grasshoppers can hear sounds that humans cannot hear. Some **species** of grasshoppers do not have ears. These grasshoppers rely on smell, not sound.

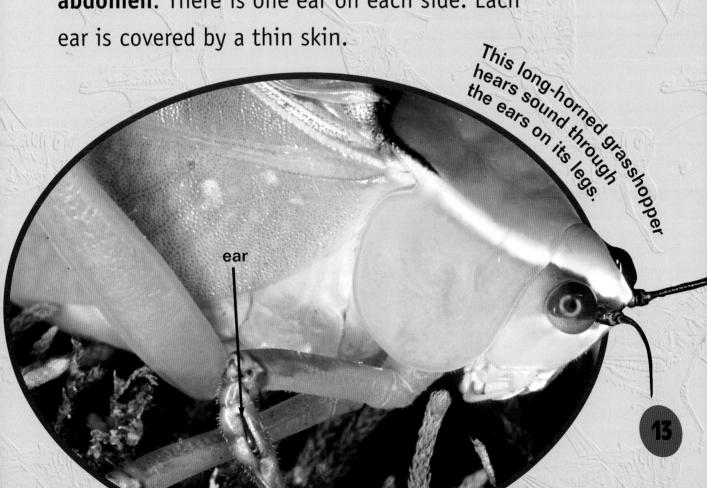

ear

This long-horned grasshopper hears sound through the ears on its legs.

Antennae and palps

Taste and smell are important **senses** to a grasshopper. They tell it if its food is fresh. **Species** of grasshoppers that have no ears need a sense of smell to find a mate.

Antennae

Grasshoppers use their sense of smell to find fresh shoots. Grasshoppers smell with their **antennae**, or feelers. The antennae are made up of tiny parts, so that they can be waved in many directions. When a grasshopper waves its antennae, smells are picked up by the antennae.

A grasshopper cleans its antennae with its front feet. It must keep its antennae clean so new smells can be picked up.

Palps

Palps are the four finger-like mouthparts on a grasshopper's head. The grasshopper uses its palps to taste its food. The palps also move the food to the grasshopper's mouth.

When this grasshopper bites off a piece of leaf, its palps pass the food to its mouth.

palp

Legs and wings

When you think of a grasshopper, do you picture its long hind legs?

Legs

Most of the time, grasshoppers walk. This saves energy and helps them to hide from **predators**. If a grasshopper needs to escape, its powerful back legs allow it to leap away in a flash.

Feet

A grasshopper's feet are hooked so that they can grip grass stems. Long-horned grasshoppers also have sticky pads on their feet. These help them to grip plant stems.

hooked foot —

Wings

Some grasshopper **species** have a pair of back wings and a pair of front wings. Others have back wings only. Some species have no wings at all. Grasshoppers use their wings to make their jumps longer. Only **migrating** locusts, which are a kind of short-horned grasshopper, fly long distances.

Legs for digging

The sand grasshopper of Australia's deserts has wide middle legs that scoop sand away. In this way, it can bury itself out of sight of predators.

Most grasshoppers can only fly for short distances.

Inside a grasshopper

Grasshoppers have clear blood and a heart that is shaped like a tube.

Blood

A grasshopper's blood moves through the spaces in its body. The blood travels from the head, through the **thorax** and into the **abdomen**. From there, the heart pumps it forward again.

How do grasshoppers get air?

A grasshopper does not breathe through its mouth. It gets air into its body through tiny holes called **spiracles** (spi-ra-kels). There are about ten spiracles down each side of a grasshopper's body.

Brain

A grasshopper's brain gets information that it senses through its **antennae**, eyes, ears and **palps**. It sends messages to the rest of the grasshopper's body about what to do.

What happens to food?

When a grasshopper swallows, food passes along a tube and into the stomach. As the food moves, it is broken down to release **nutrients**. A grasshopper needs nutrients to stay alive.

Dry droppings

Waste passes out through the grasshopper's anus. A grasshopper's droppings are very dry. This helps the grasshopper to save water.

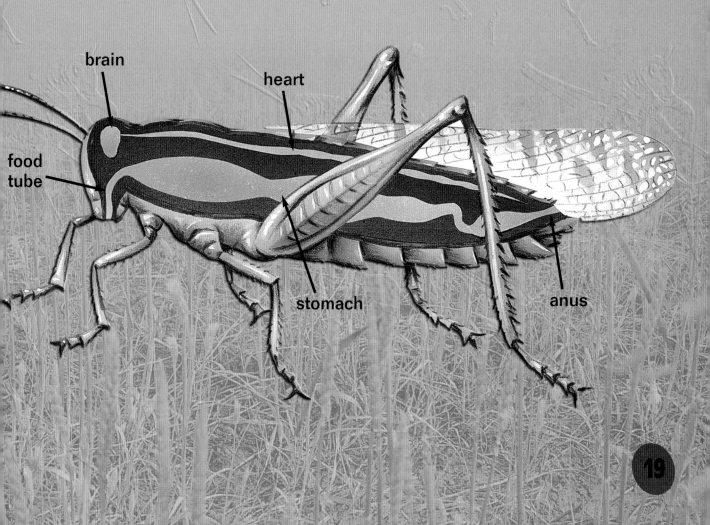

brain

heart

food tube

stomach

anus

19

The life cycle of a grasshopper begins when the males sing to attract females. This usually happens in late summer.

Calling females

Male short-horned grasshoppers sing by rubbing one of their large jumping legs against the side of one of their wings. Male long-horned grasshoppers rub their wings together. Male grasshoppers that do not have wings give off a scent to attract females.

This male grasshopper is singing by rubbing its back leg against a wing.

Mating

Female grasshoppers release smells to let males know they are ready to **mate**. When a female has chosen a male, the two grasshoppers mate.

Fighting

A male grasshopper can be quite energetic when trying to attract a female. If other males get too close, he may jump at them or wave his **antennae** wildly.

When short-horned grasshoppers mate, the male climbs onto the female's back and holds on with his legs.

Laying eggs

A few weeks after **mating**, female grasshoppers look for places to lay their eggs. Eggs are laid through a tube called an **ovipositor**. A female pushes her ovipositor deep into soil or a plant stem. When the hole is deep enough, she lays her eggs.

This katydid grasshopper is laying her eggs in a plant stem.

ovipositor

Eggs

The eggs are long and thin and laid in rows. A foamy **liquid** also comes out of the ovipositor. This foam keeps the eggs moist. When the hole is full, the female covers it with soil.

Long and sharp

Long-horned grasshoppers have very long ovipositors. They are also very sharp and can be used to cut into rotten wood, plant stems or hard soil. It is in these places that long-horned grasshoppers lay their eggs.

Locust eggs are laid in soil. A locust is a type of short-horned grasshopper.

23

Young grasshoppers

Winter comes and the weather is cold. The grasshopper eggs are well protected in their holes. When spring arrives and fresh new shoots begin to grow, the eggs hatch.

Nymphs

When a young grasshopper first breaks through the eggshell, it looks like a worm. But in an hour or two, it loses its skin. Then it looks like a tiny grasshopper. At this stage, it is called a **nymph**. The nymph crawls out of the nest hole.

These young grasshopper nymphs are on a leaf.

Growing up

A nymph feeds on leaves and shoots, and grows quickly. But its skin, or **exoskeleton**, does not grow. Soon it is too small for the nymph. The old exoskeleton splits. This is called **moulting**. The nymph then crawls out of its old exoskeleton with a new exoskeleton already formed. While this new exoskeleton is still soft, it stretches to fit. In a few hours, the new exoskeleton will harden. The nymph then eats its old exoskeleton.

This nymph has just moulted.

old exoskeleton

Pest grasshoppers

Most of the time, locusts live like any other short-horned grasshopper. They feed in one area and their numbers are not high. But sometimes there can be lots and lots of locusts in a big group called a **swarm**. Then they are called **plague** locusts.

Forming a swarm

Sometimes, many locust eggs are laid in autumn. If most of them survive over winter, millions of **nymphs** will appear in spring.

These nymphs feed quickly and soon their food runs out. To get more food, they have to move elsewhere. When they grow wings and become adults, they form a huge swarm.

There may be millions of locusts in a swarm.

Locust plague

The **swarm** takes off and flies across the land. It may travel 400 kilometres (about 250 miles) in one night, if the wind is right. If the swarm settles on a wheat crop, it can eat it to the ground in a day. The swarm has become a locust **plague**. If the locusts run out of food, they starve to death.

This wheat crop has been damaged by locusts.

Grasshoppers and us

You can learn a lot about grasshoppers by keeping them in a jar with some grass stems.

Most of the time, people do not seem to mind grasshoppers.

Perhaps the only people who get upset about grasshoppers are farmers whose crops are destroyed by a locust plague.

By watching the weather, scientists can work out when large numbers of grasshopper **nymphs** might appear. Spraying with **insecticide** kills the nymphs before they become winged adults.

Find out for yourself

Summer is the best time to watch grasshoppers. You may see and hear them whirr into the air as you walk across a field. You may even hear males singing to attract females. Look among the leaves of bushes. You may see a long-horned grasshopper climbing about.

Books to read

Living Nature: Insects, Angela Royston (Chrysalis Children's Books, 2003)

The Life of a Grasshopper, Clare Hibbert (Raintree, 2004)

Using the Internet

Explore the Internet to find out more about grasshoppers. Websites can change, so do not worry if the links below no longer work. Use a search engine, such as www.yahooligans.com or www.internet4kids.com, and type in a keyword such as 'grasshopper', or the name of a particular grasshopper **species**.

Websites

http://insected.arizona.edu/ghopperrear.htm   Find out how to raise grasshoppers in the classroom or at home.

http://www.enchantedlearning.com/subjects/insects/orthoptera/grasshopperprintout.shtml   More facts about grasshoppers, plus a picture to print out, label and colour in.

Glossary

abdomen   last of the three main sections of an insect

antenna   (plural: antennae) feeler on an insect's head

bask   lie in the sun to warm up

compound eye   eye made up of many parts

exoskeleton   hard outside skin of an insect

habitat   place where an animal lives

insecticide   poison that kills insects

liquid   something that is runny, such as juice, not hard

mandible   jaw

mate   when a male and a female come together to produce young

migrating   moving from one place to another, often over a long distance

moult   when a growing insect splits open its exoskeleton and climbs out of it; many insects need to moult so they can grow

nectar   sweet liquid inside flowers

nutrients   parts of food that are important for an animal's health

nymph   young grasshopper

ocelli   small eyes on a grasshopper's head that sense light

ovipositor   part of a female grasshopper used to lay eggs

palp   finger-like part of a grasshopper's mouth

plague   huge number of locusts that cause damage to crops

pollen   substance on flowers made of dry, dusty grains, usually yellow

predator   animal that kills and eats other animals

sense   how an animal knows what is going on around it, such as seeing, hearing or smelling

species   type or kind of animal

spiracle   tiny air hole

swarm   many insects moving together

thorax   chest part of an insect

Index